# ... And No One Knew

BRENDA A. JORDAN

# Table of Contents

# Introduction

This story is being written to encourage and uplift those who have experienced abuse, as I have. My goal is to let you know as you read my story that there is life, a fulfilled life, even after abuse.

I pray that these words I have penned from my experiences will help to heal you from your brokenness.

"The miracle is not in the life that I lost, but in the life that I've got".

# ... And No One Knew

BRENDA A. JORDAN

# Chapter I

## My Childhood

I WAS BORN IN A SMALL TOWN (at that time) on the east coast, outside of Baltimore, MD. I was the youngest of four children at the time I was born, but my mother later had more children. My father was not in our lives when we were growing up. I was told by one of my older sisters that my father would often leave my mother, then he would come back. Each time he came back, my mother would get pregnant. The last time he left, I was told, my mother was pregnant with me. I was told that my mother was living with my grandmother (her mother), and my grandmother was tired of my mother having babies.

So, my grandmother told my mother that she had to find someplace else to live.

During that time, my mother met my stepfather. She was six months pregnant with me, and she had my two older sisters and my oldest brother (who is now deceased). I was told that my stepfather took an interest in my mother and moved her and my three siblings into a house in a rural area.

I remember us moving into the house. When we got there, I saw paint cans in the middle bedroom. The house needed a lot of work. There were three bedrooms: One off from the living room, one off from the dining room, and one off from the kitchen. There was no electricity or indoor plumbing. So that meant we used an outhouse.

The house was a dilapidated, dark place. It was standing on cinder blocks on all four corners. You could literally walk underneath the house. There were cinder blocks for steps.

My second-oldest sister, Suzie, decided to mix all the paints one day. According to her recollection, there were three different colors: One white, one blue, and she can't remember the other color. Suzie took a stick that was in the white paint and stirred it, and then she took the stick with the white paint on it and put it in the blue paint and swirled it around. She was fascinated with how the white paint made swirls in the blue paint.

When our stepfather came home and saw what Suzie had done, he gave her the worst beating. I believe that that was the beginning of many beatings for us.

One day my brother, who is now deceased, decided to play "barbershop" with me, and he cut off all of my hair. I think I was about five years old. My brother and I were about two years apart in age. Suzie informed me that our mother gave my brother and me some scissors and magazines to keep us busy because it was a rainy day. That's when my brother decided to play barbershop. He cut all my hair off as I stated before, so much so that I had to wear a hat for months until it grew back. I think my brother did me a favor, because my hair grew back long and pretty. I don't know where my mother was while we were playing barbershop. She was probably asleep. My mother did sleep a lot.

The area we lived in was considered "rural" (country). There was no electricity or indoor plumbing. It reminded me of a farm. There were chickens, pigs, ducks, rabbits, and we even had a goat. I hated where we lived and how we lived.

I remember there was a pump out in the back of the house, a few feet from the back door. Since we didn't have indoor plumbing, we had to prime the pump. That meant we got a cup of water from the rain water we stored and poured it down the spout of the pump and kept pushing the handle of the pump up and down. When the handle started getting tight, that meant the water was coming up from the well.

We used lanterns for light. We did our homework by it, and used it to go outside to use the toilet at night. We didn't have toilet paper, so we would rub newspaper together until it got soft. That was our "toilet paper". Sometimes we used brown paper bags.

I don't remember much of my childhood from ages 4-9. It's very vague. I do remember, however, when my stepfather would come in drunk and start arguing and fighting.

I remember when I was around ten or eleven years old, and my mother was in the kitchen washing clothes, and my stepfather started hitting my mother. I ran out the house; it was very dark. I was running up the small hill, and there were no street lights at that time: there were only dirt roads.

I ran to a restaurant up the road.  All of this occurred back in the days of segregation. The people in the restaurant were all white. They asked me what I was doing there. I told them that my stepfather was beating my mother. One of the people then told me to stay right there while they called the police. When the police came, they put me in the back of the car and took me to the house. They asked me where I lived, and I showed them. Back in those days, we were always taught to say, "Yes sir", "No sir", "Yes Ma'am", and "No Ma'am" to all adults. When the police got to the house, my stepfather had his hand raised to hit my mother. The police took him to jail.

He was there for a couple of days. I was so happy. But that didn't last long. My mother went and got him out. I was so angry with her. When he was in jail for those couple of days, we had the best times that I can remember. My mother told us that it was just going to be us from then on. That didn't happen. I felt that my mother had let me down.

As years went by, things got really bad. My stepfather continued his drinking, and there was always a lot of arguing, yelling, and screaming. I was a very nervous child.

I do not for the life of me remember when the other four children came along. I do remember however, that a baby was sleeping in a bureau drawer because there was no crib. Suzie told me that it was our baby brother, who still lives today.

I remember one time we were all sitting around the table in the dining room and my stepfather came home drunk. His mouth was bleeding and he was mad. He went in the front bedroom and got his shotgun and left out the house. He said he was going to kill somebody. I think my mother tried to stop him, but he pushed her away.

As years went by, things worsened. My stepfather would come in drunk and start fussing about any little thing. When he would come down the hill in his beat up truck and his hat cocked to the side, we knew we were in for a rough time. He would come in, and I was so scared. All he had to do was call my name, and I thought my heart would jump out of my body. He would tell me to get him a glass of water, or fix him a bologna sandwich. I would shake like a leaf on a tree. My mother would get upset with me because of how nervous and scared I was.

I remember when he would beat us with a razor strap. He would make us strip down to our underwear, and he tied us to the metal mattress and beat us. I can't remember what he beat us for. Sometimes, just because. I'm trying to remember where my mother was during all these horrible times. I guess she was asleep, or just ignored it. There was no such thing as a box spring and mattress. Or, at least I had never heard of it or saw one until I moved away.

There was a wood stove in the kitchen and one in the dining room. My stepfather would go out early in the morning to chop wood for both stoves to start a fire to get us warm. I always thought he only did that for his own children. But the rest of us did reap the benefit of the heat from the stove.

I do not remember when my younger brothers and sisters were born, or even when they were infants and toddlers. I draw a complete blank when it comes to that time. As I remember, there was no love or affection shown to me when I was growing up. I never heard the words, "I love you" during my entire childhood. There were no hugs or pats on the back, telling us we'd done a good job at something. It was always, for me, fear. I was so unhappy.

I remember my mother having an old Wringer washing machine. We would pull the machine out from the back bedroom when it was time to wash our clothes. My stepfather made a type of closet for the machine to go in. The washing machine was stored in the closet throughout the winter. During the summer, it was stored outside in the backyard on a makeshift patio. Of course back then, I had never heard of a patio.

He put a line up in the kitchen to hang the clothes to dry during the winter. It would take very long for our clothes to dry. Especially those old blankets that were given to us. Sometimes I went to school wearing damp clothes. We had to dress in the cold if my stepfather had not gotten up to get the wood before we got up.

My stepfather had a cruel way of waking us up. He would pour cold water down in our ears. He would also sometimes put a dead mouse in my shoes, and when I put my shoes on, I could feel the mouse. He would laugh. I never thought it was funny. I always felt that he was an evil man. Especially when he had been drinking. There were times when we had to run to a neighbor's house for safety as a result of his actions.

# Chapter II

## Winter's Blow

WINTERS WERE VERY COLD, and we always had a lot of snow. The wind would howl, especially at night. It was creepy. We didn't have blankets to keep us warm. We had to use coats as blankets. Suzie shared with me that there was a time when we had nothing to keep us warm. I don't remember that. I do remember, however, that there was a family friend who drove a truck for a moving company and that they used heavy blankets to cover furniture they were transporting. He gave us some of the blankets to keep us warm.

When it came to food, there were many times that we only had mayonnaise sandwiches, or syrup sandwiches to eat. The name of the syrup we used was called King Syrup. Many times we went to bed hungry. Sometimes during the winter, we had to go to the "outside" toilet in the dark. We took a lantern with us. We would go two by two and each wait until the other was finished. It was brutally cold during those days. I hated being in that house. I never remember us having gloves. My stepfather would go outside and chop wood for the stove to warm up the house. Sometimes we had to wait until the wood burned a while before we could get warm. I believed it was cheap stove, because when the wood started burning, the stove would turn red from the heat.

Sometimes, it was so cold in that house that I could see the vapor from my mouth when I breathed. Since we didn't have plumbing indoors, and we had to hang wet blankets in the kitchen, my stepfather would put sugar on top of the stove so we couldn't smell the urine.

We did go out and play in the snow sometimes. When we did, we used socks for gloves. There was a big sled that could hold about five or six of us. The neighbor's children would come and sled with us. To be honest, that was one of the only times I remember having fun. I never remember being able to laugh as a child. Some people would ask my mother, "Why doesn't she smile?" I don't know what my mother's response was.

# Chapter III

## School Days


**Elementary School**

*School days, school days*
*Dear old golden rule days.*
*Reading and writing and arithmetic.*
*Taught to the tune of the hickory stick.*

*You were my Queen in Calico.*
*I was your bashful Barefoot Beau.*
*You wrote my slate. I love you Joe.*
*When we were a couple of kids.*
*Those were the type of songs we sang in those*
*days.*

*Daisy, Daisy, give me your answer do.*
*I'm half-crazy all for the love of you.*
*It won't be a stylish marriage- I can't afford a*
*carriage,*
*But you'll look sweet upon a seat of a bicycle*
*built for two.*
*Michael, Michael, here is your answer true.*
*I'm not crazy for all the love of you.*
*There won't be a stylish marriage, if you can't*
*afford a carriage,*
*Cause I'll be a switched, if I get hitched on a*
*bicycle hitched for two.*

THOSE WERE SOME OF THE INNOCENT SONGS WE SANG in elementary school. Unfortunately, I did not like school at all. You would think with the songs we sang, it would make for a happy childhood. It did for fleeting moments, but I was always wondering what would happen when I left school to go back to that house.

In school, I remember I had to stand in front of the class to recite the multiplication table. When I would miss some of the answers, the class would laugh at me. That's when I became embarrassed. I developed a complex after that. If I was called on for anything, I would get knots in my stomach. That still holds true today.

One day in elementary school, I remember I had to go to the bathroom. The bathrooms were outside. It was very cold. When I came back in the classroom, I shivered and I said out loud, "Brrr, it's cold outside!"

My teacher made me go outside and get a switch (a thin twig or stick used for whipping), and bring it to him.

He stood me in front of the class and hit me on my hand with the switch several times for talking. That was another moment of embarrassment. It stung so bad that my hand turned blood-red. I drew my hand back due to the pain, and the more I drew it back, the harder he hit me. I was wincing, but I did not cry in front of the class. I cried when I was walking back to my house. I remember seeing the faces of the other children. Some laughed, but some had tears in their eyes. One of my classmates, who walked home also, caught up with me and asked me if I was alright. I told her I was, but I really wasn't.

I didn't say anything to my mother when I got home, because if my stepfather heard about it, I would get another beating. I believe I was in the fourth grade at that time, so that would make me about ten years old. I never considered myself smart because I was always told by my stepfather how dumb and stupid I was with my 'yellow' self.

I remember in elementary school, we celebrated something called May Day. In the month of May, we all had different colored strips of crepe paper and we would dance around the flag pole, draping the pole with the beautiful colors of the crepe paper. I guess you could say that was another fun time for me. As we covered the flag pole we sang, "All Around the Flag Pole". We sang it to the tune of, "Pop Goes The Weasel". It was an annual celebration. The school enrolled children in grades one through six. The next level was seventh to ninth grades, which were called junior high. The tenth to twelfth grades were called senior high.

**Junior High School**

We walked to school every day. Rain, snow, or sleet; it didn't matter. It was about a mile and a half to two miles each way. I didn't have nice clothes to wear, so I was laughed at a lot. I was embarrassed going to school because I had to wear my oldest sister's shoes. Her feet were two sizes smaller than mine, so you can imagine walking a mile and a half one way, what that did to my feet.

I remember one day when I was in school, we went on a field trip. We had to bring our own bagged lunches. I sat in the back of the bus because I was too embarrassed about the lunch I had. All the other kids had different kinds of sandwiches, fruit, cookies, chips, and drinks. When some of the kids came back to where I was sitting, they asked me what I had for lunch. I did not want to show them. One of them grabbed my bag and saw that I had a greasy fried egg sandwich. They laughed at me all the way back to school. No one came to my rescue. I guessed I should have been used to that, because no one ever came to my rescue during childhood.

Back then the word "bully" was never used. I never even heard the word until I became an adult and had my own children.

I was very light in complexion and had long hair. When I walked from school, a group of girls always picked on me. They made fun of my clothes. They would pull my hair. They would shove me. I was so scared. I never fought back. I thought I could get some relief from the fighting and cursing at the house where I lived by going to school. Instead, it seemed like trouble followed me everywhere I went.

I never had any real friends in school. I would hear the kids talking about spending the weekend at their friend's house. I never asked any of my school mates to come home with me.

I remember when my mother would send me to the store. My stepfather gave me a certain time to be back. If I wasn't back by that time, I would get a beating. I learned to walk fast. As a matter for fact, I still walk fast. I don't know how to walk leisurely.

During those times, we as Blacks had our own community. We had our own stores, barbershops, fish markets, cab companies, and hair salons. We had our own doctors, dentists, and our own movie theater, even though there was only one. We all went to all Black schools with all Black educators. We didn't have to go out of our community for anything.

# Chapter IV

## High School

I DIDN'T LIKE HIGH SCHOOL EITHER, because I was afraid that I wasn't smart enough and I would get embarrassed again. There was one class that I really liked, and that was called P.E., or Physical Education. I was really good at that. I could climb the ropes and mount the horse, which today is called the balancing beam. At one time I wanted to be a P.E. teacher. During those days, our class schedules were listed like this: 9A-9B-9C, and so on, depending on the type of classes you were taking. It went that way all through high school.

I was impressed with my oldest sister so much that I wanted to be like her. She took all academic classes. I should have taken C-classes, which meant learning to type, or to be a secretary. C stood for Commercial Classes. I did everything my sister did when it came to the classes I chose. She went on to college to become an elementary school teacher. She was the first in our family at that time to attend college. I had aspirations of going to college, but no one encouraged me or pushed me in that direction. I did graduate from high school and received my diploma. I found out later in life that I was not as dumb or stupid as I was led to believe. I believe that discouragement was one of the reasons I didn't pursue higher education.

I did have two best girlfriends in high school. We were together all of the time. The other students called us the Three Musketeers. We were inseparable. You wouldn't see one without the other two. I had the privilege of spending some weekends in "the country" with one of my friends. It was great! I didn't realize before visiting with my friends that some families actually had fun together, not fighting, or yelling, or arguing. They had a large house and a lot of land. They always had people visiting, having fun, and always had plenty of food.

My girlfriend who I will call "Robbie", we would hang out in her bedroom. She had a vanity table with mirrors. We would sit on the bench in front of the mirrors and sing. My sisters, Suzie, Marlene, and I would sing all the time. We were a trio and we would go all over the area to different churches to sing. My mother played the piano. We even sang one time on the radio. When Robbie and I would sing in front of the mirrors, however, I would tell her to stick to her academic skills. We shared a good laugh about that!

Robbie and I had so much fun. That was the only time I got the opportunity to ride the yellow school bus, because my brothers and sisters and I always walked to school. When I spent time with her family, I also felt peace: I didn't have to hear yelling, cussing, and screaming.

I never invited my friends to visit me at the house where I lived. One of several reasons was that I was embarrassed of where I lived. The other reason was that I didn't know when *he*, my stepfather, would be drunk.

## Times of Fear

Suzie got pregnant and had a baby at sixteen years old. Those days were horrible. Why do I say horrible? Because my stepfather tried to kill Suzie and her baby. Let me explain. First of all, the house we lived in had windows that were low in the back of the house. One time he (my stepfather) tried to chop the bedroom door down where my sister and the baby were.

While he was doing that, my mother and I got my sister and her baby out through the window so they could escape. That was so scary. Another time, he poured pepper on the hot wood stove in the kitchen to smoke her and the baby out. The bedroom where my sister and her baby stayed was off from the kitchen. The wood stove would get so hot that it turned red.

I asked Suzie where she and the baby went when we got them through the window, because I don't remember. She told me they went next door to one of our neighbor's houses.

There were many times that my stepfather would do such evil things. I remember one time we were sitting at the dining room table eating, and I was picking up my fork and holding my little finger, which was called the "pinkie finger", out straight and he accused me of trying to be "proper".

"You think you're better than everybody else!" he yelled.

He took the handle of a butter knife and hit my finger with it. I don't know if it was broken or not, but it went limp. It began to swell. I never went to the doctor to see about it. When he saw that it was swelling, he told me to put some ice on it. Back then we had what we called an "ice box", which is now called a refrigerator. There were no ice trays like we have today or ice makers. We had blocks of ice delivered by the "ice truck". They would put it in the "ice box"/refrigerator, and when we needed ice, we would take an ice pick and chop the ice.

Another scary time was when I was around twelve or thirteen years old. My mother sent me to the store with a list of things to get. She called a taxi cab. They couldn't come down the hill because they would get stuck in the snow. It was dead winter and snow was on the ground. So, the cab driver would blow his horn to let us know he was waiting. I walked up the hill and got into the cab. He waited for me until I was finished getting the things on the list my mother gave to me.

As the cab driver was taking me home, he began to ask me questions.

At that time, I didn't understand why he was asking me such personal questions like, "Do you have a boyfriend?"

I said, "No sir".

"Have you started your monthly yet?"

"No sir". We were always taught to "no sir", "Yes sir", "No ma'am", "Yes ma'am".

I really started getting scared. My heart started pounding because I was really feeling uncomfortable with the things he was asking me. I was sitting in the back seat. The cab driver started driving behind a warehouse building. He stopped the car and began to reach back toward me. I opened the back door of the cab, threw the money on the seat, took the bag of groceries I had and ran all the way back to the house in the snow. It may have been about three to five inches of snow. During those snowy days, they never closed stores or schools. We also never had anyone to come and clear the streets like they do today.

When I got back to the house, I told my mother what happened. She told my stepfather, and he called the cab company and reported the driver. Of course, I told them who the man was because at that time it was a small town and everybody knew everybody. I never found out what happened to him.

That was one of many sexual assaults against me. My stepfather had a brother, Jimmy, and he would come to the house to visit a lot. One time in particular, when I was around eight years old, Jimmy came to visit. I don't remember where everybody was. But Jimmy came into the kitchen and said to me,

"Come here, girl."

I went over to him, and he sat me on his legs. He began to fondle me. Then he put his hand down my pants and begin to put his finger in my private part. Then he made me kiss him and he put his tongue in my mouth. That was awful.

I told my mother, and you would not believe what she said. "Oh! He didn't mean any harm."

Even though I was just eight years old, I felt like I was not protected by my mother. I think her response to that incident was the beginning of me believing that I could not trust or believe anything my mother said. I felt a sense of bitterness toward her, but I still loved her because she was my mother. And we were always taught to respect our elders. Maybe that's what it was rather than love – respect - because I never knew what love looked like.

No one knew that I was afraid all the time. No one knew how afraid I was in school because I didn't want to be embarrassed if the teacher called on me for the answer and I didn't get it right. No one knew how scared I was walking home from school and getting punched, my hair being pulled, and being called foul names. I never told my mother about those times. Why? Because she would more than likely say, "Oh! They didn't mean any harm."

Unfortunately, the incidents I described were not the only times that I was sexually assaulted.

I recall going to the post office one day to get stamps and to mail my mother's bill payments off to their respective companies. I did that on several occasions, also going to the grocery store several times. There was a man there who I knew, and he was well known in the community. He told me to follow him upstairs where he could get me faster service. That worked well for me because I had to be back at a certain time, or else I would get a beating.

Being naïve as I was, I followed him. He closed the door behind me, threw me on the table, covered my mouth with his hand so I wouldn't scream, pulled my skirt up and my underwear down and got on top of me and put himself in me. It was painful and I bled a lot. Afterward, he gave me some tissue to put in my underwear.

I went into the bathroom to try to clean myself up as much as I could to stop the bleeding so my mother nor anyone else would be able to tell that anything was wrong. He told me if I said anything that he would deny it and I would be put in jail for making up such a story. So I never told anyone.

There was another incident with the same man. I was coming from the store getting ready to catch a cab to go to the house. He pulled over and said, "Get in; I'll take you."

I said, "No."

He said, "You better get in, or else."

I was scared, so I got in, but he didn't take me home. He pulled into a wooded area. It was all woods where we lived. I did not recognize where he was taking me because I was so scared. I knew what he was going to do.

He had a friend with him also, and I knew him as well. He brought his friend along as a lookout. He got in the back seat where I was, pushed me down in the seat, and had his way with me. This time, I didn't bleed. I had enough sense to know that I was no longer a virgin. He took me to the house. I got out and went inside. No one noticed that I was upset, or even asked who the cab driver was.

I really felt that no one cared. I don't remember who was in the house when I came in, with the exception of my mother, and she was probably sleep. It was many years before I told anyone about this. I told my two older sisters about it later on.

It is so interesting and disturbing looking back and remembering how we all lived in the same house for years, and none of us knew about the molestations and the rapes that the others had encountered. We were all threatened to be hurt if we ever said anything. When my sisters and I got together later on in life, however, we began to share our experiences that we went through.

# Chapter V

## About My Mother

MY MOTHER WAS A WOMAN WHO LOVED GOD. As children, we went to church all the time. We never missed a Sunday, and we always went to Sunday School. My mother played the organ and the piano for years. She was the organist at her church for over four decades.

I do remember a period of time when we would go to church, and my mother at the time was not going. She always sent us to church, even when she wouldn't go herself. We went to a Methodist church, and my grandfather (my father's father) was a lay speaker there.

My mother, according to Suzie, didn't start going to church until she began playing for a group. Plus, she didn't always attend the same church we attended.

I don't know a lot about my mother's growing up years. I only hear pieces of it when my older sister and I get together and we talk about our childhood, which was never pleasant. I know that my mother loved her father. She was a daddy's girl. My grandmother (her mother) was not a very affectionate person. I know that there was never any affection shown to me by my mother. Perhaps the reason for this was that there was no affection shown to her by her mother. I really don't remember much about my mother except what my sisters tell me. All I can remember is her being in church a lot. Looking back, that could have been her way of escaping from the violence and the turmoil she endured.

Through the years, I learned to love my mother. What does the word love mean to me? Strong feelings of affection and devotion. A strong liking. I became very devoted to my mother as she got older and I got older and began to understand about life and the choices she made. I believe that my mother did the best she could for us. Looking back, I am grateful to her to this day for showing us what a Godly woman is, and leading all of us to the Cross.

At this very moment that I pen these words, all of my siblings have a deep relationship with Jesus.

My mother, in her later years, taught us about the love of God. I too can say that I have love toward God. Strong feelings of affection and devotion.  I attribute this to my mother.

My mother's health began to fail as she approached her seventies. She had cancer of the bones and the breast. We, her children, decided that we would not put her in a nursing home when she became gravely ill. Suzie quit her job to take care of our mother. We all took turns helping out. When I got off from my job, I would come to relieve my sister. We took turns staying overnight. When my mother came home from the hospital, hospice came. They were so devoted to my mother. She passed at home. That was over twenty years ago. My siblings and I talk about our mother all the time.

When we were growing up, when I went to church I would always hear the preacher talking about God our heavenly Father, and how He loves us. I would think to myself as a young child, *If He is so loving, why does He allow my stepfather to beat us and mistreat my mother?*

For years, I had a very hard time believing that God, who I had never seen, could love me. I could not relate to God being my father because the two men, my father, and my stepfather, who were supposed to love me and care for me, were non-existent. So, how could I trust someone whom I've never seen to love me?

Back to my mother - as the years wore on, I learned to care a lot about my mother. I remember the times she would be in the living room playing the piano and she would call us in there and she began to play and she taught us to sing. I found out later that we all had a talent and gift of singing. I was an alto, Suzie was a first soprano, and Marlene was a second soprano. We began singing at early ages. We became a trio and we sang in area churches.

Suzie explained to me a few more things about my mother: My mother went to church regularly with her father, because he sang in the choir. He attended the Methodist church we attended. He was a baritone and he was really good. I believe that's where my mother got her musical talents from. As a result, we too inherited that. I don't ever remember my grandmother (my mother's mother) going to church, but she always sent her dues, which we now call tithes. Back in those days, we were never taught about tithes.

My mother graduated from high school and went to college in Virginia. She completed four years. On graduation day, she was not allowed to walk across the stage to receive her degree because they found out that she was pregnant. But we do have her degree to this day.

My mother was a kind person. She would give her last to someone in need. Many times she would go without to help someone.

Suzie tells me a lot about my mother. I am three years younger than her, so she knows more than I do. She shared with me about my mother's giving and helping others. One time, one of our neighbors asked my mother if she had an extra pair of stockings. Back then, there was no such thing as "pantyhose". There was only one color for us colored folks, and it was called, "Red Fox". My mother only had one pair, but she gave it to our neighbor. Suzie said that our mother came home, took a can of Hershey's cocoa powder, used a powder puff, and covered her legs with it to replace her own stockings.

I felt that my mother's kindness was to a fault. I understand not being selfish and extending to others more than yourself, but, I don't believe we are to go without to show the love of God. God gives us wisdom to discern.

# Chapter VI

## About My Father

I REMEMBER MY FATHER BEING A VERY HANDSOME MAN. I was so proud being his daughter, although I didn't grow up with him in my life. I remember him being a referee at our high school football and basketball games. My classmates knew he was my father. Whenever he called a foul or whatever, they would always look at me. I was so proud of that.

The sad part was that he never acknowledged me. I would run up to him after the games to say hi and he would say, "Go away young lady". That was so humiliating and embarrassing, because I was giving the impression to my classmates that I had a great relationship with my father. He never in all my years, even upon his death, did he ever call me by my name. It was always, "Young Lady".

I remember when I was a teenager that I had to go to his mother's house, who was my grandmother, every Thursday to pick up the child support money he had to pay for the four of us, which was $13 a week. I'll call my grandmother "Grandma C". She was always there when I would come. And she was always upstairs in her chair in her bedroom.

I would yell out, "Grandma C, it's me!"

She would say, "Hi baby; how you doing?"

I would say, "Fine, Grandma C".

Then she would respond, "Come on up so I can see you."

I would go up the stairs and say hi and give her a hug. I had to hurry up and leave.

She would ask, "Why are you always in a hurry?"

I would reply, "I have to get back home".

She didn't know that I had to get back in a hurry because if I wasn't back by the time my stepfather said to be back, I would get a beating.

I am, as I pen these words, in my seventies, and I still walk fast.

Back to my father: I was told that he was a womanizer. I do know that he had been married three times and had children from each union. He also became a preacher and a Pastor. My two sisters and I would always go across the Bay Bridge to his church on Father's Day to honor him as our father. He even christened my children when they were babies. That's what they call it in the Methodist denomination. I felt like it was a joke to go to his church on Father's Day, because he never really acknowledged us as his children.

The interesting piece of this is, two of my older sisters had a relationship with him. He would always say that I was the "peculiar one". I had so much pent up anger toward him for not being in my life as a child.

As years went by, I stopped looking for validation from my father. I never stopped loving him though. That was the strangest thing to me. I never thought he loved me.

I remember a time when we, my two older sisters and I, went to see our father. We decided to confront him and tell him what our lives were like as children and ask him why he never wanted to be in our lives. Well, in my opinion, it ended disastrously.

We poured our hearts out to him and there was no reaction at all. After that, I got up, walked to the door and left. I said that I was done, because there was no remorse.

I did however, eventually forgive my father for not being there for me. The next time I saw my father after that day was at his funeral. I must say, the only sadness I felt was that he didn't take advantage of the many opportunities to get to know me. I felt that it was his loss.

## My Exit from my Stepfather's Home

After all of the fear and abuse that I endured as a result of my stepfather's actions, he eventually kicked me out of his house. I believe I was put out because my stepfather realized that he could not get to me sexually.

I met my now husband when I was fifteen. We started dating. I stayed out past my curfew, and my stepfather became upset. As a result, he started calling me a slut and accusing me of being sexually active, which at the time I was not.

After this went on for a period of time, I was told that I had to leave his house.

# Chapter VII

## Where Is She Now?

WHERE IS THAT LITTLE GIRL that was raped, and physically, mentally, and emotionally abused? The teenager that was put out of the house at age fifteen?

What happened to her? Well, let me tell you where she is, and what her life has been like over the years since she left home.

When I was put out at 15 years old, I went to live with my oldest sister and her family in a two bedroom apartment. I slept on the couch for two years. But let me back up a little bit. Before I left my stepfather's house to go live with my sister, I met a guy who was stationed at the United States Naval Academy.

He was not a midshipman; he was a medic.

I had heard about a dance in town. I must have asked my mother if I could go because we were not allowed to do anything without asking.

I remember going to the dance, and this guy had on a sailor's suit. He walked up to me and asked me to dance, and I did. He had a friend with him, and his friend got sick, so my now husband had to take him back to the base.

Before he left, he kissed me on the cheek and said, "I'll be back." I didn't see him for at least six months.

One day, I was coming from the cleaners and he spotted me. We talked for a few minutes. He was a pretty good looking guy. He dressed really nice when he wasn't wearing his uniform. I was going on 16 years old at the time, and he was 20 years old. Back during those times, sailors had a bad reputation. When they would come to town, the majority of them would only be in town for a few weeks.

During the times I didn't see him, he was in training at the Bethesda Naval Base. He was there for three months. After his training, he came to the Naval Academy for almost two years. During those times, I would sneak to see him because I wasn't allowed to date.

One day, my mother was hanging up clothes on the clothes line in the backyard, and I asked her if my now husband could come to the house. Her response was "Absolutely not". That's when I started sneaking to see him.

My mother finally said he could come to the house. I was totally embarrassed. We had no indoor plumbing. We had wood stoves.

He didn't mind. He took me to my prom at age seventeen. I knew then that he was the one for me.

It wasn't long after us dating that I was put out of the house and I had to go live with my sister and her family. I graduated from high school at seventeen. I married my husband at eighteen. I had my first child at nineteen.

During the time that all of this was happening, I was very much still a child myself. I had no life experiences except molestation, rape, and physical abuse. I felt my husband was my knight in shining armor. I felt like he rescued me from all the trauma I had experienced.

I didn't realize until much later that I was looking for a daddy. Not a father, because I had a father and a stepfather who did not cover me.

I now have three adult children who I dearly love. I have ten grandchildren, four great grands, and I had a daycare business in my home for twenty years. God really blessed me to train up children in the way they should go. I was very successful in that business. Not so much financially, but in imparting into children ages two to five to prepare them for kindergarten, elementary, middle school, high school and college. I must say that the majority of the children that I worked with have completed college and are now in their careers. Most of them are still in touch with me. I am so proud of them. They are my successes.

My husband and I have been married for sixty years. There have been many bumps in the road for us. I have to say that my husband has always been and still is a wonderful provider, and a wonderful father and grandfather.

So, as I close this story, I love the Lord. In addition to everything else He has done in my life, He has also gifted me to be a minister of the Gospel of Jesus Christ.

I want to encourage others, male or female, that there is life after abuse.

*"The miracle is not in the life that I lost, but in the life I've got."*

God Bless whoever reads this book.

In His service,

Brenda A. Jordan

PS: God can reach down and heal our brokenness.

www.ingramcontent.com/pod-product-compliance
Lightning Source LLC
Chambersburg PA
CBHW061441050726
47593CB00004B/1413